Making New Friends

By Linda Cernak

Scott Foresman
is an imprint of

Glenview, Illinois • Boston, Massachusetts • Chandler, Arizona •
Upper Saddle River, New Jersey

Photographs

Every effort has been made to secure permission and provide appropriate credit for photographic material. The publisher deeply regrets any omission and pledges to correct errors called to its attention in subsequent editions.

Unless otherwise acknowledged, all photographs are the property of Pearson Education, Inc.

Photo locators denoted as follows: Top (T), Center (C), Bottom (B), Left (L), Right (R), Background (Bkgd)

Opener: ©Mike McGill/Corbis; **1** Jupiter Images; **3** ©bilderlounge/Alamy; **4** ©Jonathan Kirn/Stock Connection/Jupiter Images; **5** ©John-Francis Bourke/Getty Images; **6** altrendo images/Getty Images; **7** Jupiter Images; **8** ©Nicholas Prior/Taxi//Getty Images; **9** ©Baerbel Schmidt/Stone/Getty Images; **10** ©Mike McGill/Corbis; **11** ©Mike McGill/Corbis; **12** Jupiter Images.

ISBN 13: 978-0-328-47260-4
ISBN 10:   0-328-47260-3

7 8 9 10 V010 16 15 14 13

It's moving day! All those hours of sorting and packing are finally over. Everything, down to the last paper clip, is packed in a box. All the boxes have labels that tell what's inside.

Movies

Shirts

Pants

Carefully, the movers carry boxes and furniture into the van. You go back inside for one last look at your empty house. How are you feeling about this?

Your family is in the car. They honk for you to hurry up.

No one says much on the trip to your new home. Each person is wondering, *What will it be like in our new town? How will I make friends?*

The first day in your new home might be confusing. You can't find your favorite jeans or your toothbrush.

But little by little, everything turns up and you find a place for it all.

Your parents meet the neighbors. You notice there are a couple of kids your age on your block. You think maybe it's a good idea to invite them over to see your stuff or play a game.

It's the first day at your new school! You get lost trying to find your classroom, but everyone is very helpful. Finally you find it. You meet your teacher and look for an empty seat. You wonder, *Will any of these kids be my friends?*

Then it's lunchtime. The lunchroom is a lonely place when you're the new kid in school. The first day, you eat by yourself, just taking it all in. You feel as if the other kids are looking at you.

After school, you walk home. You notice a few kids on skateboards. Later, your mom takes you to the skateboard park. At last, you start to feel comfortable in your new town. You *really* know how to skateboard!

At the skateboard park, you see a girl from your class. She comes over to say hello. She tells you about a skateboard contest in a few weeks. She asks you to help her with her jumps. You smile and say to yourself, *I think I'm going to like it here!*

Maybe moving isn't so bad after all. You can stay in touch with your old friends and make lots of new friends too!